the heart's Viceroy

the heart's Viceroy

collected poems on love, loss, and liberation

r. tyrel london

dedication

For friends, family, and friends who are family.
Thank you for the love and light you have blessed
me with.

table of Contents

for barbara larae

The clouds wept in my stead:
They knew my job must well my tears,
And feeling my heavy heart,
They could not help but ache for you

Perhaps the greatest sorrow is found
In all the life we did not share;
That's always the regret—
In not seeing enough,
Calling enough,
Loving enough;
But these regrets we bury, too;
I cannot change, now, the way we lived,
Only the fervence with which I now remember

A piece of you runs on in all the lives you leave,
Passed on through the love you made:
That's perhaps the greatest miracle
Of God's great and glorious creation;
Your blood runs through my veins,
And so you, too, live on It's your voice I'll miss the most;
I could live another hundred years
And still wait for another strong and lovely lady
Whose sound is just the same;
I am left in the quiet,
Hanging on the world to sing,
Like you, a pony boy lullaby

I'm sorry to all the answers
To the questions I should have asked,
For I meant to set them free upon the world;
But there is something

Exquisite
In their exclusivity;
A finality of it all—
What was yours is yours,
And you get to take it with you in the wind;
You lived your life, every second of it,
And now it's still yours as you return
From where you came:
Dust,
Blowing in a cool mountain breeze,
With family smiling, crying, loving
The hell of a woman you were

For it is our duty—
the son, the daughter, the kin—
To lay to rest those who woke us
from our once and future slumber;
It is **the order of things**,
In all God's seasons,
For ends to follow beginnings,
And for them, too, to end

And so you go on before us
to the last great journey;
The mansions of rest await,
Open armed,
Aching to ease the aches
a full life bestowed you;
I will see you there,
at long last,
When it is my turn in the order of things

Until that day calls me home,
Enjoy your rest, dear love.

the Viceroy

r. tyrel london

The world's my oyster
I'm allergic to shellfish
This is a sad poem

the heart's Viceroy

A chain echoes across barren meadows.
The empty gourd waits, watches, listens.
A raven ripens, ready to be picked.
A man enters and then exits again.

Rattled breath haunts the ground
As thoughts turn food fowl,
foul fog, nipping night.

Halt! Who enters, exits, struts about.
Whimpers from beyond the rock.
Halt! Enough. I yield. I give.
Give the gourd my grave
Give me to the vine
The skeleton rattles.
Or is that the breath?

Halt! Who moves? Who asks?
Who. Who. The owl turns the raven turns the mouse.
Who. Who. Struts and turns and walks about.

A candle darkens air to ash
The night burns bright
In my core, aye, in my heart of heart.

Passion's slave? He's connected to the vine.
The grapes grow near for spicéd wine.

Is that you, Hades? Old friend? Godot? Haven't heard of
him.

Are we to reunite? Again?
Is this rest? This gourd that tightens at the neck
Behind the rock. This will be the death of me.

Hello? Hello. I know this place, this field, this darkness.

3

r. tyrel london

Ah, yes. Now I remember.
Echoes echo across the rock.

The vine tightens. The raven caws. The gourd fills.
The moon shines blood as blood deigns darkness.
No grave here. The rattles seize and cease.
The full gourd rolls *blindly into the night*.

the heart's Viceroy

Yours is a face not even a mother could love,
Yours is a body not even a cannon would fodder.
You aren't worth the words.
I've dreamed up villains worse than you

-this mirror called life

r. tyrel london

Even now I feel it.
That long dark night
Of my last supper
when I prepared the hammer
to drive the nails
into my wrists
And let death rattle out—
clumsy like the life it followed.

Even now I feel it.
That same dark terror
mapping a better world without me,
Without the pain I had caused,
the pain I lived through.
It tugs at me to tenor the world toward its breast:
to end it all,
better it all
with my erasure.

Even now I feel it.
That last noted scribble
In trembling script,
The last letters on a page
Burdened with the last of my hurting
Unloading it on a family
Who would learn to heal better
Without me.

Even now I feel it.
That dreadnaught lord
Whose tainted steps
Creak in every crevice
Of my body:
A body sinking from too much sadness.
I cannot escape,
mirrors everywhere,

Or is it water
Cutting like glass,
Whipped by some foul substance
that needs no name.

I am on land
I am drowning

But even now, I dream of walking
Through the flowing wheat
Of Elysium
The wind peacing my face,
Licking my wounds.

As I gasp now for breath
I crave the noose
I never made
For the tree I never visited
At the grave I never dug.
I'm searching for answers
in *this, my intimate darkness*

Even now I beg.
How do I escape?

Still I find
no answers. only pain.
…paralyzing pain…
Each breathe battles the millennium of and in a moment
How long can a sinking ship float?
How long can a heart beat against the current?

Even now I feel it
Echoes on a stormy sea
Taunting my arms as I try to pour
out the water that salts my wounds.
Even now I feel it.

r. tyrel london

You were my first love,
and I was your last.
You tutored me in **the oldest art**
beneath moss-smelling vines
of a willow no longer alone in her weeping.
Our roots, the tree and I
might wind along the river's bend,
but that shadowed spot
is yours now. You stole it from me.

How many nights was it both of ours?
Between that first grumbled hello
in a breaking down pickup truck
to when we last fogged up my rearview mirror?
I think we saw the moon molt thrice
in the gloried heat of our summer passion,
ignoring the pests in our tree and lives,
pretending we were more substantial than the wind
that tickled the leaves above us.
We didn't understand
three leaves falling was
a tarot:
the universal sign
of star-vexed lovers destined
to burn too brightly,
and in their brightness, burn.

Will you visit me, sometime,
beneath the willow no longer lonely,
a boy
far too intimate with loneliness
for one whose skin is still pocked
by youth's coming of age.
If I lay enough tears on that spot,
will you, like the flowers of a summer
after a wet and misty spring,

sprout forth from this long,
unbearable winter?
Won't you return? Return?
Return.

It doesn't work like that,
does it?
No rewind,
Redo,
Replay.
Return. Return. Return. Don't you still have that get out of
jail free card
tucked between a Trojan and an Amex
In your calfskin leather bifold?
Or is it all Monopoly money to God in the end?
A feckless thug. That's what he is.
I'd say she, but I've yet to meet a woman
whose eyes are sharpened
by the blood of boys
He made foreigners
in the place they should be
least foreign.
God needs a therapist, a hobby, something.
Can I say that,
or will I be smote?
That doesn't sound so bad. I promised I would follow you to
the ends of the earth.
Maybe I just follow you to the end.

No.
It doesn't work like that,
does it?
The world is as it is, and I cannot
change the terrible landscape of the past
no matter how calloused I make my fingers
by praying beads through them.
They aren't seeds,

I'm no farmer.
But neither is God,
or at least not a good one.
Because right now my landscape is barren,
You stolen from me
Because the world you were placed in
Was too rough for your soft soul.
The world couldn't keep you safe,
And fuck, I'm sorry for that.
I'm mad that God
would make you soft in a hard world.
A feckless thug.
Loamy soil.

No.
It doesn't work like that.
We are our fate,
our fields as filled
as we plant them.
Samuel Hamilton
tamed even his soil:
God isn't the farmer.
I am.
I am.
I am.
The brag of my heart
is the requiem of yours.
Am I Job?

No.
It doesn't work like that.
I am not a sadist's betting block.
We, fickle humans, we.
Pretending, attributing, blaming, excusing.
Chaining our goodness
and our badness
to the world:

the heart's Viceroy

No back is strong enough to carry the cross
of knowing we are all of us Christ and crucifier.

This is our doing,
all of us,
me,
you,
we, fickle humans, we
chose to do what we did.

I chose to fall in love,
to invest my heart
in a soul that didn't invest there itself

And you chose to leave.
 This privileged history wasn't enough for you,
so a revolver replaced me on your lips,
the wind your final lullaby.

r. tyrel london

I can feel it sitting in my throat
Whatever this thing is
I feel water swashing and pushing
As the muscles swell together

I cannot breathe
Whatever this is
It is choking me
Wringing tears from my eyes
Comfort from my chest
Beats from my heart

I am scared
Whatever this thing is
Not screaming-to-the-void,
Praying-for-a-savior scared.
Paralyzed.
Utterly desolated
In the face of whatever this thing is

The light cannot touch it,
Even as it blackens my blood

the heart's Viceroy

I dreamed of you
As morning danced the clouds away
And the stars rained a memory.
We waltzed to dreams as lovers do,
All while I dreamed of you.

A blanket wrapped about me,
Like the sun birthed on the sea.
I sang a tune that we both knew,
And we danced on whispered dreams.

You bit my neck, I kissed your nose,
And the dark of days gone by
Were days gone by.

And we were there.
And we were whole.
The flutter of a moment lasts a lifetime.
A single breath that spanned our breasts
Took us home and filled our longings.

A coffee cup, for me.
A cup of tea, for you.
One spoon of sugar poured in each,
The bliss of us within our reach.

And so I reached.

I see you now, as we were then.
The careful tomes we told
became our story.
A great good bye
Was our surprise,
A secret fate I did not know.
Did you know then
what I know now?

r. tyrel london

We would never kiss like that again,
No more holding me as days turned evening,
No finding ourselves lost in dreams
Of you
Of me
Of us
They, like our days gone by,
Are days gone by.

And now I know the past
sinks away and the lights
are shifting. I am far
beyond my cue, but still
I feel it moving:
Some great design
cogging along,
without my feigning heartbeat.

I break alone,
While you seem fine.

But will I go?
For still I dream of you.

Do you dream of me?
No. We are not to be
And still. And still. And still.
I dream of you.

I dream of you
Like the stars greet evening
Like the stars that fade to morning.
I take a step on the clouds
held up by dreams
 and move towards the horizon of self.
We converge at the rising.

the heart's Viceroy

Reality replaces memory,
And I see the day gone by.

A yellow rose on a blue table:
Our final goodbye.

GrindrGay420 asked: looking for?
Someone to stop my looking.
my soul is hiding
until something different comes along.

the heart's Viceroy

You'd think by now I'd be the expert
at loneliness, that silence and I
are intimate acquaintances
But it's really like those awkward
car rides with a long-lost aunt
Where you know it should be comfortable

But it's not

r. tyrel london

Can we quit
trying *to finish ourselves*
with other people?
their pieces
have yet to fit
my puzzle,
and I cannot
remember where they start
and I end.

the heart's Viceroy

Is that a fat joke?
Yes,
if you keep **looking for a villain**,
you will eventually find one.

r. tyrel london

my bones are the type of tired
only old people should know;
sadness got in somehow,
and now there's no getting rid of it;
life is losing its luster,
and I must learn to live
when I ache in *all the wrong places*

the heart's Viceroy

a stranger
pressed naked against me
him: a flint
then: a spark
scene: a moment
illuminated intimacy
exposing my exposé
treating me as my own villain.

-questioning my manifesto

*t*his poetry isn't vegan

Perhaps it's best I never find you:
I would move the sun to give you shade,
Empty countries to give you peace,
Slaughter a feast of lambs and chicks and cows
If you so much as mentioned a craving.
I would flatten mountains and terrace hills
To help you walk the world,
Reorganize the cosmos
To write your name in stars,
And still it would not be enough
To give and show and love you
With all I am and can and could be.
So I would go on until all was gone,
And the Gods,
Rather than lose their Olympian seat,
Have cast our fates beyond the four corners of the world
To opposite ends of time and space.
Only the taste of you in my dreams remain
As the tantalizing reminder
From the Chairman of the Gods:
Epic love stories are too powerful for truth

the heart's Viceroy

Eating away my pain hasn't work,
it brings more pain.
Eating toward happiness hasn't worked,
it brings more pain.
Eating for comfort hasn't worked,
it brings more pain.
Maybe I should stop looking for answers in things made from wheat.

r. tyrel london

You're the man, I'll find out sometime soon
the man who walks past with a scarf-swaddled neck,
his gayly-paced gait the melody
that scores a dream of mine

i tumble in the field where the late daisies bloom,
the aspens painting the wood
with the light of the golden hour,
the tint the sun shares but briefly
in the quick turning times of fall

and as i roll,
the crescendoed patter of your feet
tilt my head toward the first verse
of an ongoing love letter

your scarf forms and falls
with the beating of the wind.
periwinkle, you say sometime soon,
works well with your complexion.
it leaves with the leaves,
the sky in the sun;
but you let it go
falling to our bed of daisies

and just as you call me over,
i wake up
and look out the window
to see the walk of the man
whose world is galaxies apart
from my own

i feel a stranger,
marked apart
from the harmony
we call love;

the heart's Viceroy

gays, you say sometime soon,
are worthless without abs

your scarf tightens,
the door closes,
 and i hear you chuckling
as you walk away
"too good at pictures for his own good
i couldn't love him, *not even in his dreams*"

r. tyrel london

I miss the feeling

of your tummy
pressed on mine,
when my stretch marks didn't taunt me
because your body embraced them

of the moments
in between our words,
when silence didn't need filling
because silence said it all

Three dates
Then you loved me
Two kisses
Then you loved me
One sleep
Then you loved me.
One fight
Then you left me
Two heartaches
Then you left me
Three months
Then you left me.

Funny how *we made a circle*:
completing each other
even in our separation.

The last time
our bellies pressed
against each other
you asked me not to leave,
but I had other life to live.
If I had stayed,
would you have done the same?

I doubt you even cried
while my heart broke in places
it did not know it had

the heart's Viceroy

I touched the place between your eyes
And we stared into the other's souls.
I saw stars where only freckles were,
just like I saw love where only titillation was.
Our hair tickled the other's,
Both brown, like our eyes.
Your nose touched mine
In an intimate sort of sweaty;
August kissed us
More than we kissed us.

But still there was not an inch of ourselves
We hid from the worship of the other.
In that moment, we were one.
Even now my heart quickens,
Thinking of the taste of you
In the hanging air of summer,
Thinking of your voracious appetite for me
That seemed boundless.

We found its bounds.
In that infinite moment
We were galaxies onto ourselves.
And when the moment ended,
Words left my mouth
Where your kisses used to come.

r. tyrel london

I picked each one,
The florist blushing to see a boy
So interested in flowers.
Each petal I weighed
Against a platonic form:
Only the perfect bouquet for you.
Wrapped. Ready. Roses.

Yellow, like the song I sang to you
The first night my lips met yours
And in so singing sealed it ours.

Yellow, like the sun we watched set
The first night my tummy pressed on yours

Yellow, like the stars above
The first night I truly serenaded you
As we danced on the grass.

Yellow, like a coward,
As they sat rotting, wilting,
Weeping like me.
You wouldn't come get them
You wouldn't look me in the eye
So I left them by the statue
That witnessed our first kiss,
Called it a requiem of the delusion
Coming out, being out
Was possible in our time and place.

Your fear proved me wrong,
And tears rock me to sleep
Instead of your heartbeat

the heart's Viceroy

In the dark—
When I pray for sleep to come
And yet another prayer goes unanswered—
I close my eyes.
Another time, a different journey:
the place I ache to be.

The fields of Elysium,
The ones watered
With the lifeblood of my soul

I run, faster than my feet have ever known.
I fly, higher than soul has ever touched.
The grass ripples freely, doing its dance with the wind.
The place where I wait for the sleep to come

it never does come

the grass falls flat
the still wind shrieks
i, motionless, fall
toward something
no longer elysium

Dreams never could save me
Love never would touch me. No cure
For strife filled
Aching life
Aching to be free
Aching for that field waits for me.
And I call it home,
the final rest,
home:

is that place
Elysium?

r. tyrel london

Pissing in the shower was your guess
When I tried to intimate you with me.
You farted on me
The first night you slept in my arms
 And I wanted you to know
Something basely human about me, too.

So I told you my strange fascination
With cleaning the lint from my bellybutton,
Hoping it might help you love me.

But you did not see like me,
No cleaning of the original well spout of my creation
Muddied by life outside the womb.
You saw insignificance.

I had naively hoped
Shared intimacy,
However trivial,
Was a goodwill foundation for love.

I was wrong,
 And now this is the shower
And you are the lint.

***writing
cleans my soul of you***

the heart's Viceroy

What if i can't
what if i never do
what if the weight stays, the boys leave, and i am left.
alone.
what if my best is not enough,
and i fall short despite growing all i could?
what if i can't be the hero of my own story?

what happens the day i wake up and realize
my dreams won't come true?
the sweat i poured from every pore
fell onto the seeds of hope
i planted
with every book,
with every burpee,
with every breath.
and still nothing came.
the emotions surpassed
my minds capacity,
forced themselves out
as tears,
watered the field of my hopes

and still i face a desert

what happens the night i feel my last moment coming
the purple tint of evening
glinting across millennia, eons even,
lighting me, alone,
in a faded flannel
on a faded porch
with a faded face.
is this when the prayers come
or when i realize prayers dissipate into nothingness
just like me

r. tyrel london

what moment matters
in this ticking tilt of eternity?
what war is worth winning,
when all the power in the world
might still lose

where do i go
when i've traveled the world
and found that all my life
and work
and love
and longing
is weighed at last
and at last found wanting

will i fade like the smaller stars do—
smaller and smaller
until everything else around it ends.
supernovae are reserved
for the real stars,
whose gravity reached
critical mass at critical moments.
and however hard i've tried,

i am not one of those stars

i am one who
lauds the evening breeze
with weighted odes
to speak memory into myth,
and the one wanting to go with them.

and yet i am
as the wind all the same
dissipating against a mountain
i will not see fall.
it will crumble eventually,

just not by me.
i could be a hurricane,
but the mountain sits nonetheless.
and i'm not a hurricane,
not even the grass bows to me.

no one will sing me into eternity
no heart will beat for me
when mine beats no more.
what happens then?

what happens when all is for naught,
when hope was a folly,
when it is done,
and i have done it all,
given every fiber of my soul
to find there is nothing left to give
and nothing left to have.
do i keep going past all that?

what if i can't?

r. tyrel london

I like to think
that given the chance
I'm one of the mistakes you'd repeat

the heart's Viceroy

I'm sorry someone convinced you
That you had **to close your heart**
To make it whole.

I'm mad the world fooled you
Into calling boarded windows and brick walls
love.

r. tyrel london

there are days where i want to take
the knife that cuts up the food
i gorge on until bursting
 and cut off the sides that i have stuffed
take the blade and sculpt
make me the david
to pay in blood and flesh
for the pain i have felt
the pain far more real than
blood and flesh
i want to take a knife
and lop off limbs
until i feel whole

darkness does that

the heart's Viceroy

Your garden's shit
Because you don't tend it
At some point
It's no longer the world's fault

-you can't blame the world for everything

the heart

the heart's Viceroy

Get your life together.

Love,
Another Fuckup

r. tyrel london

I will love you something galactic:
Bigger than constellations and memories and histories.
They will have to tread lightly on this story
For fear my love will outshine the ages

-the long-awaited letter to myself

the heart's Viceroy

does the rain fall so sweetly
as where we know we can dry ourselves
after dancing in it

I won today,
even though I dragged myself from bed
And skulked to the gym.
You didn't want me to leave,
But depression,
Life isn't all about want.

the heart's Viceroy

Make yourself
into the person you want to be
Run the marathon
Lift the weights
Sweat away the idea
You are unable to live
A vibrant life
Filled to pouring over
With all the glories you need

r. tyrel london

These are my *stigmata*,
Inked wrists of mine own choosing
Self-inflicted pains that remind me my essence
Of choosing to continue
And choosing to believe.
What better way to live and love is there?

the heart's Viceroy

I can't say I realized,
because I didn't.
not one
iota
of whom I am
acquiesced to my will.

And yet *I willed it anyway*.
I chose
not to give my love
to anyone who shouldn't have it

r. tyrel london

I'm sitting here, done
with classes but not the semester.

I felt loved today by **the boy who broke my heart
yesterday**.
The love he stored in me,
during our two-month love affair,
wrapped me in a glorious, gentle, glowing way.
I am loved
and safe
and sexy.
I am not too much or not enough.

His memory kissed me and whispered, ever so tenderly,
that I can face this challenge too.
He wasn't lying when he said he loved me,
but giving me light didn't leave enough for him,
and when you love somebody, when you really, really love
somebody,
you make sure they have enough for themselves before
taking.

This breakup hurts in a nostalgic way,
not because it was wrong,
but because it was right
but the timing was off and it wasn't in our fate and however
hard you try
sometimes fate wins.
And that's okay.
We each have before us a destiny.
And we can and should fight those parts that should not be
ours to bear,
but sometimes you lose those fights.
And when you lose
you remember
that you've won before

the heart's Viceroy

and you take out a piece of the light
you made with that winning.

And dating him,
that sure was winning.

And we made light together,
and today I got to see it and see the world by it

and isn't that lucky?

But damn.
Using light hurts a lot more than making it sometimes,
and this is one of those hurts.
Glorious but gory,
the mangled pieces of my heart find respite in their
destruction.
Can a heart break too many times?
Will it stop fixing?
Maybe hearts never mend,
maybe they just have more places for the light to get in

Before the tyrant time
takes us to the tomb eternal
Let us be us,
lively, whole, alive.
Love something fiercely
 Before it all falls apart,
And we fall apart with it.
To cry:
This is the summer of my liberation,
the year the chains
are broken and cast aside.

I am free to love myself
In all my faults and frailties,
To kiss my own wounds
Into the fertile soil that grows
the flowers I owe myself.

After a lifetime of mything me and unholy
Into some modern Medusa,
I stand, feet wide, on the cliff of my fate
And now I jump
To fall or fly,
Both endings deliciously mine.

Being is the gift I grant myself
And never will the sun rise again
On a divorced self.
I will take me
To the place I started,
Returning once more,
dust and dust again.
And until the dust, I am I.
Until my death, I am I. I am I.

the heart's Viceroy

For one day soon
From the epics of my life
The sinews in me will fail.
But until they are dust I walk
The mountains will crumble
But until they are dust I walk
The sands of time
Will one day run out
But until they do I walk
I walk the mountains
And valleys and the hillocks in between
I walk the beaches and oceans
And ride the waves my feet ripple
In the place no longer and not quite dust.
I walk as dust among dust,
Stardust made earthdust made me,
And one day dust again
In the cosmic winds of starlight.
And then I'll take the dust remaining
And blow it from my hand
into a new world to walk once more

And from that dust a spring
And from that spring a river
And from that river an ocean
And from that ocean, life.

Stardust will always be stardust,
we are just lucky enough to know
all our beings are made
from the same cosmic explosion
as the constellations dotting our dreams

My body will return to dust
After I have used every last iota
Of its strength
The grave will greet me

r. tyrel london

With kisses to my scars and stretch marks
My brief moment in the sun
Will notch freckles onto me,
With which I now count these cherished days.
I need not be afraid
Of the ragged signs of living:
Only a fool tries to escape life alive.
I will greet my end as I greeted my beginning,
In a moment of ecstasy and love
Transcending our small bounds

the heart's Viceroy

I hope you are a star
And not a moon.
That you **radiate yourself**,
Not glow from someone else's light

r. tyrel london

The greatest hope is a tree planted
A seed watered
A field sown
In gifting the ground tomorrow
Knowing it will grow

the heart's Viceroy

I was deeply afraid
Of the unforgiving memory of history.
To be forgotten as the sun spins round and round
Some galactic center
That isn't me.

And then, when I quieted Ego,
Dear Heart quoted that hard-won Sage, Wisdom:
Some epics are meant to be lived
and then to be known no more.
This is one of those.

How do you dissect an atom bomb?
A neutron star?
A black hole?
How can unmaking be making?
Degilding, shining?
Doing nothing to do it all?

I have found my religion.
Her name is justice
And mercy
hope
And love
equality
And peace—
God without her
Is no god at all.

Faith is found
where we do not know,
So use humility
Or lose all
In some conquest for power.
feed soul not ego:
We see what we look for,
Such is our fatal flaw.
So let us look for the good,
And anything without the good
is not what we search for,
But what we sift through.

Thrust out
into the wilderness of soul
The desert of our desserts
Where our soul rips apart,
Turning sand to glass
Magnifying the sun of self

the heart's Viceroy

With its galactic fractals
Outlining where we puzzled ourselves together
And can puzzle ourselves together again.

Life starts where fear begins
This place does not feel enough, now.
And now I know
I should not stay where I have stayed
Nor where to go when at last I go
but nothing is no option now.

No, no option indeed.

My brother is as my father was
But I am neither he nor he.
I am a mixture of both and beyond
Of what is and is not and might be
If only someday hope sprout reality
In rocky soil red
like Arizona clay
formed human formed me
With the breath of some spirit
Who flamed eternity into a heartbeat
Kept alive by the love of thousands.

But even here is not home:
What do I take with me?
What do I leave behind?
That magic of yesterday is no more:
I cannot touch it again,
Even with the help of infinite tomorrows.
But I will take tomorrow's magic in stride
As its own irreplaceable.
I will one day lament its passing, too,
Only to be confronted by some other infinite.

57

r. tyrel london

Poeticisms are not enough
In this arid desert heat.
They cannot sum the unsummable
Nor touch the untouchable.
There is too much for words,
And such is when words are most needed.
Perhaps they are grains of sand
And enough of them will fill the desert
And we will belong to the infinite.
The soil is not as red
As my Arizona home
And that is fine: here is not there

and yet they're the same, all the same.
Just me, the wind, and God
And the occasional mountain view
In this not so desolate place.

The wind lapping my face
Waltzes with the kufiyah on my head.
Theirs is the truest romance,
A pure give and take
In a place some see
As neither give nor take.
The tidal trot of the camel
Matches the beat of my heart.
Yes, small quiet voice,
This *is* what I need,
The place painted technicolor tans.
There is no thought in me
As I pass these sandstone jetties
Afloat in an ocean of sand.
This is the most ancient song,
And I am now part of it.
The dust I am and was and will be
In the place that held
the patriarchs,

the matriarchs,
And all the ancestors in between and outside
Categories not made by the mountains
But imposed on them.
The red soil native to my soul
Follows me forever,
Even to here,
Where faces, arms, and blood
Are the only shades of red.

And then I know the wilderness of our origin
And the wind of our religion,
No longer needing to pour forth
Sands and poems and trite phrases
In this holy land.

The stars show God,
And all here wait in ecstatic expectation.

the sun does not ask
for permission to shine,
thank you very much

the heart's Viceroy

the sky opens
the sun smiles
the heart sings
the soul remembers
beats, breaths, beats breast
a thousand smiles fall on wearied shoulders
as moments become minutes become memories
happiness is as the sun
always returning after the night

Pretend
you chose the world
to be as it is.
right now.
Own it, and in owning it,
free yourself from the need
to have a different starting place,
free yourself from thoughts
that do not make you strong.
it's the doing that matters.

the heart's Viceroy

Let go
like a leaf on a river
Let expectation
flow away with the tide
Let your wishes
cascade into the sunset.

Out beyond
Is the wholeness we need.
Like a sunrise on a cascading sea,
Let your life *be*:
No more nor less
Than what it is.

r. tyrel london

Write a love letter to yourself today
Write in bold *with your body*
The warmth and kindness
You have denied yourself
You are so worthy of love
That the stars shine brighter by it

Thank you to a body
That has a thankless job
Of holding, creating, sustaining
A soul
weary beyond its bounds

Thank you for eating
Even when I didn't want to

Thank you for forgiving
The purgation that can never cleanse me

Thank you for the thousands of miles
Thousands of days
Thousands of sunrises
That you have seen me through

Thank you for being stronger
Than I thought I could be
By taking me through the moments
I never planned on getting past

Thank you for taking breaths
long after I wished you had stopped

Thank you for taking up again
the reckless cause of living,
especially when I wished you wouldn't

Living is a thankless task
And you do it so well
For that, I am forever grateful

Oh heart,
What happens when you let go?
Life is found in the moments
between falling and flying

the heart's Viceroy

She said, go to the water.
So I did, and there was that place
Where mountains stretched down
And I did not know which way was right
Where three days of solitude above the alpine were
deliciously mine
She said, ask it for help,
So I did, and I saw you ripple,
And in the raising and lowering
Of your stilled breathing,
I felt the bray of my heart.
She said, let it show you,
And I did, seeing ice
In circles and seasons,
Adding and subtracting
Through the multitudes.
I asked, how do I change?
You said, show up
And *lean into your vicissitudes*.

Stop searching yesterday for happiness.
You won't find a happy ending
In a past that didn't give you one

the heart's Viceroy

Ah, sadness, my most intimate friend.
You have sojourned somewhere,
I can tell.
You are not so bitter now:
Your suffering hints salvation
Your despair echoes hope.
There's a fullness in your cheeks
I had not noticed before.
Yours is the sadness of a soul
Holding many things in too few hands
But able to hold them, all the same.
You went to *the stars, I think*,
And looked back to us.
We were just a dot
in some far-off constellation.
Perspective brought you peace
In the chaotic cosmos of my soul

r. tyrel london

Going over a mountain
Going through a mountain
Going around a mountain
All get you to **the other side**

the heart's Viceroy

if i write enough words
will the feelings be more manageable
or just more visible?
the sun's equinox has called in spring
and now I write with purifying light.
that's just as well
nobody cleans with their eyes closed

r. tyrel london

The biggest lie
is thinking you have to start
over once you fall.
Pick up *where you are*, not where you were.
Not starting again,
But continuing forward
after a tilted spiral pulled you back.
That sounds like a much healthier idea.

the heart's Viceroy

I am done justifying
Loving myself
for the self I am.
The soles of my soul
Are calloused from their journey.
My heart hasn't rested
Since I was a youngling.
The world has thrown me
Beneath the crushing weight of waves
More times than your small mind can count:
I will not justify myself to you.
Neither my voluptuous sides
nor the girth of my waist
nor the thunder of my thighs
nor the appetite of my body
Are asking your approval.
The wolf does not cow to the sheep
And I will not bow to you.
I have found love and known belonging,
Far greater for the journey I bled of myself.
If never I touch another tummy
With the tell-tale signs of longing and lusting,
Then the world will have missed out
On its greatest love story.
If I can light the world
With love of self,
Imagine the galaxies I could fill
With my passion for the one
Who does not try to change my light.
So go and walk your little hills,
And I shall master mountains

r. tyrel london

Fat on your lips
Translates to survivor in my ears,
And I will not apologize for surviving
Or how I chose to survive.

I have procrastinated happiness
waiting for the perfect moment
when the clouds have parted
And all has been made right in the world.
But the sun shines on
Above the clouds,
and the good life starts
at the boundary between
The perfect and The real

Until all of me is happy,
the sun still shines.

What's the worst that can happen
If you forgo perfection: acceptance?
You will miss some faction of fiction
we call normal,
In exchange for that thing called life?

Being broken shows how whole you are.
What teapot does not break
When thrown from high heights?
What log does not burn
When thrown on the fire?
What child does not cry
When first brought into this hard world?
Your scars show the vigor of your life:
Wear them as the royal you are.

the heart's Viceroy

God blew glitter into the cosmos
And finished the breath with saying:
This is how you love

r. tyrel london

Humor is sorrow's perfect partner,
softening the too hard into
somewhat passable.
I told a friend
of my almost suicide
in the almost rush hour.
He said: how inconsiderate!
Trains already run too slow.
I laughed and never did jump.

there is hope in that

So now when the worst thoughts come,
I laugh at them
and make them friends.

I never did jump in front of the train,
but *I sure do laugh a lot.*

the heart's Viceroy

Be a mountain
Do not miss the men
when they stop stealing Gold
from your insides

r. tyrel london

I do not need a soulmate to be whole.
Made with everything I need,
I know love does not require romance.

Like me,
Love contains multitudes

I do not need to hear "I love you."
It is the most translated phrase.

Buckle up.
Here's a coffee.
Want a hug?
You did great.
I'm sorry.

Imagine how overwhelmed we would be
if love only took one form
instead of filling **the space
between everything else**.

Love is as the air or sun:
Everything we know comes through it

***Do** not be so small*
you only care about
the oppression of self

r. tyrel london

One, two (three)
one, two (three)
beat, beat (breathe)
beat, beat (breathe)
the heart dances
through her toil
to find grace
in the everyday tedium of being.

-the waltz of living

the heart's Viceroy

Around the corner
Love might find you
Around seven thousand corners
Love might find you
At the turning of the sun
Love might find you
At the turning of the year
Love might find you
Between joys
Love might find you
Between sorrows
Love might find you

After your life is spent,
Love will have found you.

Until then,
Enjoy *turning the corner*

r. tyrel london

Nighttime is the sun's way of saying
"I know hurt, too"
And **the moon gets to reply**
"No one is alone in their hurt."

Abba,
Ours is the condensed rhythm
Of syncopated stanzas,
Sumptuous with Pauses.
The equal of my more prosaic part
In the prolific prose I write with her
Like Dickens, substantial but verbose,
there richer with every word,
yet here, here is different.

No.
With you,
I leave room
For the wind to name
What words never could.

I hope I die
In a field of flowers
And then open my eyes
To find the same field
Grown from the love
Of some infinite eternal
And spend there the rest of forever
With the poets and prophets
The family and friends
My soul and self

- *the peace I seek*

the heart's Viceroy

It is not my job
to love you like a river,
smoothing away edges
carrying your burdens.

Nor do I need you
To wash away
mine frailties neither:

I am *an ocean onto myself.*
Do not try to change me,
But respect and fear as a sailor
The awesome might of my vastness

Love,
as the spring returning after winter,
blossoms hope
blossoms the sun
blossoms flowers
blossom people
growing something spectacular.

pink petals pushing past
conceptions of inadequate
floating, flying, freeing feelings
of love and light and infinite being.

The holes of yesterday wounding
A carnal prayer whose imperfection
Makes it all the more perfect:
Things are beautiful
Because they do not stay forever,
because they trust us
With the height of their being.
What better thing is there
than love that springs us
toward some higher height,
without needing the assurance of forever

the heart's Viceroy

I have found it,
the radical notion
I deserve to be loved.
My imperative is to wait for a love deserving of me.

-wherever you are is an okay place to be

r. tyrel london

I sit here beneath weighted vines
waiting for *the God of Multitudes*.
Poppies bloom on the outstretched field
as the olive trees grow heavy
with the burden of age.
An azure sky reaches down to kiss me,
but pauses:
this is where my holiness lives.
Room for my soul to breathe free
as I wait for a deity that might never come.
My breath beats with the tenacity of the wind:
surely returning after some long sojourn
that cooled off the soul.

milk and honey mix.
histories turn mythologies
like the grapes fermenting
in the wide barrel somewhere
off behind me.
and still i crave the sky,
the enveloping kiss of an azure god
reaching down to find me.

A tree falls somewhere off in the distance:
it is the ground's turn to eat.
My feet mix with mosaic ground,
red clay, black soil, fine sand,
together and apart
for some brief but magnificent trunk of time.

We were all wild once,
and we will all be wild again.

A wind floats freely
until it, too, breathes its last.
I know the comfort of a well-earned rest

beneath an azure sky on a shaded hill,
and that peace will be mine once more
when these little things that are not little
feed the ground like felled trees and fallen grass.

the sky has just enough clouds
for the sun to paint the heavens
some other shade of holy

Still I'm not alone.
The paths traced by the wise foot
of a mother with a tight wrapped child;
vines planted by an ancestor's hand,
to which I am now heir;
and even the sky, which sings
in colors of the soul,
was gifted me
by some hand that might not be here now.
The stars that dot my heavens
are not mine alone.
In them, I find the God of Multitudes,
who gave the vines strength to climb
and the wheat patience to grow,
who grew from womb to womb
the roamers of this once wild place
that will once more be wild, again.
The technicolor heavens
give me space
to make the vista I know I need,
and to leave it once the time has come
for other hands to tend
the land and life loaned
to my wayward traveling soul.

r. tyrel london

the heart's viceroy

the heart's Viceroy

What if I never have a lover breathe
The whisper that inoculates my heart
Against further follies with future men?
"Your lilacs bring my favorite scent with them,"
The spring winds blowing pollened affection,
Stringing hearts like sentences, placed abreast
To eye the final thread themselves.
"They tint My dreams an echo 'tween purple and plum.
You're softer, here, with moonlighted edges."

If in the autumn that's not my autumn,
I never savor the words I breathe back,
"Though fall is my favorite color, my love,
you are my favorite feeling," I'll yet yearn for you.
And I'll hate myself for that feeling, too.
The apple weighted wind ought loll drooped wheat,
Tempt the harvest to empty its bounty,
Enflame the world with the color borrowed
From leaves tinted and aged by time's sage hand
Picked from trees, gifted to ground—tumbling hopes.
It is a time for feasting and laughter,
To delight in blessings we have planted,
That the sweat of summer has grown and earned.
And yet, I'll try to add to my table-
Already pouring over with plenty-
A place for a lilac-bearing lover.

My discontent is to weather winter
Without the rush on my neck in the night
Declaring my belonging here with you.
Your breath on my skin earning your place,
Dripping with pulp born of that same flower
That fills in my doubts and tilts up my head
Toward the dance of Alaskan night
In midwinter's forever-feeling dark.
Stars abound, and there's Cassiopeia

Finding her way home through the blackest pitch.
You say to me, "Maybe we will get one:
a constellation others imitate
but, trying to, come short." We fall short,
too. You are as far away as Sparta, Troy,
Carthage, Rome. I do not see seven hills,
just seven hopes, all as momentary
as the tempting color of Northern Lights.
I do not tell my tale to you, Dido,
You are my tale and burning you will light my way.

You are not fated to be my summer,
I know this in my head if not my heart;
Those tyrants we call emotions wither,
supplanting each other like seasons, time,
and flowers. Lilacs make lousy bouquets,
and stories make lousy lovers. Life is,
I am made of fuller stuff than feeling,
and though I feel dictated differing
directions with each ticking of the clock,
The gardened flowers grow best when tended
tenderly when the rains don't fall.

You might yet come,
But that will not make you my sun and stars.
You might be as lovely as May or June,
but you're not May. For May is my August,
And my zenith cannot be someone else.
The seasons run, in tilted spirals, on
And on and go on, with us or without;
planets continue in their cosmic dance
far beyond our final number and note.
When that forever darkness closes in,
my bow must bring a standing ovation.
I don't want the critic to write harshly
how I abstained May for lack of a lover.
Let my casket hold if's bouquets for me,

the heart's Viceroy

Let regret be some other man's folly.
And though **the heart's viceroy** tightens my chest
I know I cannot wait, even for you.
I will be there, out there, my vistaed peace—
In Rumi's field where I unchained myself.

artistic acknowledgements

As Donne said, no man is an island unto himself, and no artist creates without it being in response to others. I have been infinitely inspired by Elizabeth Gilbert, Rupi Kaur, Nayirrah Waheed, Linda Hogan, TS Eliot, Maya Angelou, and countless others. Thank you for the art and magic that has kept me going through it all.

about the poet

R. Tyrel London is a wannabe wordsmith finishing his BA in American Studies and Film, Television, and Theatre at the University of Notre Dame. Raised in rural Arizona, he strongly believes in the beauty of the sun and the necessity of strong community. Throughout an adolescence of broken bones, obesity, eating disorders, and bipolar disorder, Tyrel has found, at the center of his liberation, art—especially writing. Going forward, he hopes to enjoy a life full to the pouring, all the while making art and finding love.

Made in the USA
Lexington, KY
10 August 2018